8062

$2.95 in USA

JOPLIN

ELITE SYNCOPATIONS FOR THE PIANO

Maurice Hinson, Editor

AN ALFRED MASTERWORK EDITION
AN ALFRED MASTERWORK EDITION

Alfred

SCOTT JOPLIN
Elite Syncopations

Illustration: Ted Engelbart

Maurice Hinson, Editor

About the Composer

Scott Joplin was born in Texarkana, Texas, on November 24, 1868, and died in New York City on April 1, 1917. He was the leading figure in ragtime and a man very much in tune with the times. He is widely considered to be the best of all ragtime composers—the most professional, original and serious composer of this genre. His music is finally receiving its proper acclaim in American literature. The works of Joplin include 53 pieces for piano, 10 songs, and the opera *Treemonisha*.

About the Music and This Edition

Form: Introduction = measures 1–4; **A** = measures 5–21; **B** = 22–38; **A** = 39–54; **C** = 55–71; **D** = 72–88.

Elite Syncopations, with its spicy rhythms, was composed in 1902 while Joplin was living in St. Louis, Missouri. It opens with a four-measure introduction. Measures 1–2 contain syncopation (offbeat rhythm) that is created by tying the fourth and fifth 16th notes. Consequently, the emphasis is shifted to the second 16th of the last four-16th-note group. This same use of syncopation continues in much of section **A**, measures 5–21. Joplin introduced an interesting figure in measure 4 by alternating hands, left hand first followed by the right hand. This type of figure is used in measures 7, 15, 20, 38, 41 and 49.

Section **B**, measures 22–38, adds a different syncopation at measures 22, 26, 28 and 30, by accenting the eighth note in the second half of the measure. This type of syncopation was first heard in the first half of measure 3.

Section **C**, measures 55–71, features even 16th notes interspersed with syncopation in measures 56, 60–61, 64 and 68.

Continued on page 7

This edition is dedicated to Dr. Ronald Lewis, with appreciation and admiration.

Maurice Hinson

Copyright © MCMXCIV by Alfred Publishing Co., Inc.
All rights reserved. Printed in USA.

AF876431

Elite Syncopations

(1902)

Not fast (♩ = ca. 72)

Scott Joplin
(1868–1917)

22
mf – p
27
32
37
1.
repeat RH 8va
2.
loco
f
42

47
51
55
mf
59
63
f

67
1.
2.
f
72
f
76
80
mp
84
cresc.
f
1.
2.

Continued from page 2

Section **D**, measures 72–88, features syncopation in two-measure pairs. In measure 72, the first 16th note is tied to the last 16th of measure 71, with the same rhythm in the second half of the measure as the second half of measure 22. In measure 73, the fourth and fifth 16ths are tied, followed by an eighth note on the weak part of the beat. The two-measure pairs that follow use the same or similar rhythm patterns. The harmonic change in measure 84 adds color and contrast to the conclusion of the rag.

Practice and performance suggestions:

1. Follow the dynamics carefully for a colorful performance. The ***f–p*** at measure 5 means to play that section, measures 5–21, forte throughout the first time and piano on the repeat. The same principle applies in measures 22–37.
2. Establish a comfortable (not fast) tempo at the beginning and maintain this tempo throughout the rag.
3. Keep the hands perfectly coordinated at all times.
4. A slight emphasis on the syncopated rhythm, such as the last eighth in measures 5–6, 13–14, and similar places, is appropriate.

The pedal should be used very sparingly, only touches here and there, such as on beat 1 in measures 5–6, 13–14 and similar measures, beat 2 in measure 29, beat 1 in measure 71 and the last chord in measure 88. Use half pedal rather than full (deep) pedal. The delightful rhythms will not be heard if too much pedal is used.

All fingerings, dynamics and the metronomic indication in parentheses are editorial.

Source: John Stark & Sons, St. Louis, 1902. Also available in Alfred edition no. 4615.

ALFRED MASTERWORK EDITIONS

(partial listing, K - Z)

Kabalevsky
619 24 Pieces for Children, Op. 39 (Palmer)
2486 30 Piano Pieces, Op. 27 (Palmer)
1719 First Book for Pianists (Palmer)
1734 Introduction to His Piano Works (Palmer)
1706 Sonatinas for Piano, Op. 13 (Palmer)

Khatchaturian
1711 Album for Young People, Vol. 1 (Palmer)

Köhler
567 12 Easy Studies, Op. 157 (Palmer)
628 Short School of Velocity, Op. 242 (Palmer)
1710 Sonatina Album (Small)

Kuhlau
2279 3 Sonatinas, Op. 20 (Palmer)
2277 6 Sonatinas, Op. 55 (Palmer)

Liszt
630 Technical Exercises, Complete (Esteban)

Lynes
2590 Analytical Sonatinas, Op. 39 (Olson)

MacDowell
2641 Sea Pieces, Op. 55 (Olson)
2278 Woodland Sketches, Op. 51 (Palmer)

Mendelssohn
1958 6 Christmas Pieces, Op. 72 (Palmer)
472 First Book for Pianists (Halford)
470 Introduction to His Piano Works (Halford)
468 Songs without Words (Selections) (Aldrich)

Mozart
391 21 Most Popular Pieces (Palmer)
1707 6 Viennese Sonatinas (Palmer)
384 Easiest Piano Pieces
493 First Book for Pianists (Palmer)
664 Introduction to His Piano Works (Palmer)

Pischna
500 Little Pischna (Palmer)
637 Technical Studies (Brisman)

Prokofiev
631 Music for Young People, Op. 65 (Palmer)
1743 Selected Works (Baylor)
1045 Visions Fugitives, Op. 22 (Baylor)

Rachmaninoff
536 Fantasy Pieces, Op. 3 (Baylor)
515 Preludes, Op. 23 (Baylor)
655 Preludes, Op. 32 (Baylor)
2423 Selected Works (Baylor)

Ravel
2530 Gaspard de la Nuit (Bricard)

Rebikov
1708 Silhouettes, Op. 31 (Palmer)

Reinagle
10107 24 Short & Easy Pieces, Op. 2 (ed. Hinson/Krauss)

Reinecke
2275 Nutcracker & the Mouse King, Op. 46 (Duet) (Hinson)

Satie
2501 Gymnopédies & Gnossiennes (Baylor)

Scarlatti
494 First Book for Pianists (Halford)
666 Introduction to His Keyboard Works (Halford)
108 Selected Sonatas (Hinson)
29 Sonatas, Vol. 1 (Hinson)
107 Sonatas, Vol. 2 (Hinson)

Schmitt
1709 Preparatory Exercises, Op. 16 (Palmer)

Schubert
1720 First Book for Pianists (Halford)
546 Four Impromptus, Op. 142 (Baylor)
544 Four Impromptus, Op. 90 (Baylor)
530 Impromptus, Op. 90,142, & Moments Musicaux, Op. 94 (Baylor)
482 Introduction to His Piano Works (Halford)
548 Moments Musicaux, Op. 94 (Baylor)

Schultz
1959 Scales & Chords in All Keys (Palmer)

Schumann
392 29 Most Popular Pieces (Palmer)
620 Album for the Young, Op. 68 (Palmer)
4576 Carnaval, Op. 9 (Hinson)
495 First Book for Pianists (Palmer)
483 Introduction to His Piano Works (Palmer)
4800 Papillons (Hinson)
632 Scenes from Childhood, Op. 15 (Palmer)

Scriabin
663 Selected Works (Baylor)

Shostakovich
1960 6 Pieces for Children (Palmer)
1961 Puppet Dances (Palmer)

Streabbog
621 12 Melodious Pieces, Op. 63, Vol. 1 (Palmer)
565 12 Melodious Pieces, Op. 64, Vol. 2 (Palmer)

Tchaikovsky
485 Album for the Young, Op. 39 (Novik)
4858 Nutcracker Suite, Op. 71a (Duet) (Hinson)
4856 Nutcracker Suite, Op. 71 (Solo) (Hinson)
4826 Seasons, The, Op. 37b (Hinson)

Tcherepnin
551 Bagatelles, Op. 5 (Olson)

MISCELLANEOUS MASTERWORK BOOKS
496 Early English Music/First Book for Pianists (Halford)
1987 Easy Keyboard Music—Ancient to Modern (Palmer)
361 42 Famous Classics (Small)
626 First Sonatina Book (Palmer)
1988 Harpsichord Manual (Halford)
2093 7 Centuries of Keyboard Music (Palmer)
2508 Standard Piano Classics (Small)
497 Sonatinas/First Book for Pianists (Halford)
484 Introduction to the Baroque Era (Palmer/Halford)
1732 Introduction to the Classical Era (Palmer/Halford)
2218 Introduction to Keyboard Sonatinas (Halford)
556 Introduction to the Masterworks (Palmer)
467 Introduction to the Romantic Era (Palmer/Halford)
2504 Introduction to Theme and Variations (Halford)

Alfred
Alfred Publishing Company, Inc., 16320 Roscoe Blvd.
P.O. Box 10003, Van Nuys, CA 91410-0003
www.alfredpub.com

TP
APEX
9780739014462

Joplin • Elite Syncopations • Hinson

Alfred